Published proudly in the State of Texas, USA by Xist Publishing
www.xistpublishing.com
24200 Southwest Freeway Suite 402- 290 Rosenberg, TX 77471

eISBN: 978-1-5324-4363-3
Perfect Bound ISBN: 978-1-5324-4365-7
Hardcover ISBN: 978-1-5324-4364-0

PUBLISHED IN TEXAS

xist Publishing

Experiments in Laughter

{Illustrated Science Jokes for Kids}

Stephanie Rodriguez   Brenda Ponnay

What did the limestone say to the geologist?

Don't take me for granite.

How did Ben Franklin feel after discovering electricity?

Shocked!

Why did the germ cross the microscope?

To get to the other slide.

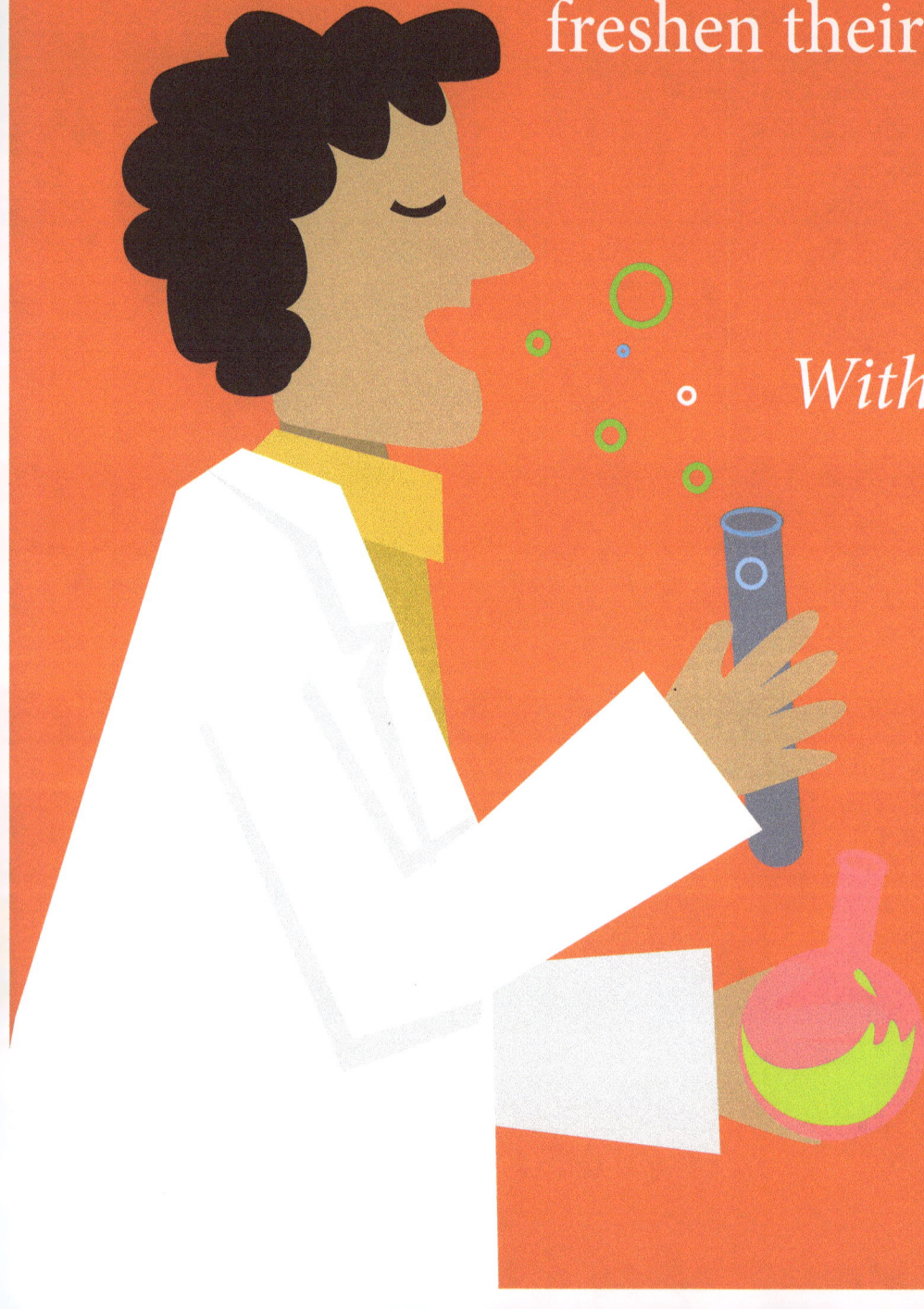

How do scientists freshen their breath?

With experi-mints.

Why did
the scientist
remove her
doorbell?

She wanted to win the no-bell prize.

What did the biologist take with the camera?

A cell-fie.

What kind of dog does a scientist have?

A *lab!*

What was the name of the first electricity detective?

Sherlock Ohms.

What is a physicist's favorite part of a baseball game?

The wave.

What do you call an
alligator in a vest?

An investi-gator.

Knock, Knock!
Who's There?
Noble Gas! *Noble Gas who?*

Nevermind,
I guess all my friends
Argon.

Why can't you trust atoms?

They make up everything.

How did Einstein begin his stories?

Once upon a space-time...

Why is electricity so dangerous?

*It doesn't know how
to conduct itself properly.*

Knock, Knock!
Who's There?
Prism!
Prism who?

It's the police!
If you don't open
the door,
you're going to
prism!

Why did hydrogen marry carbon?

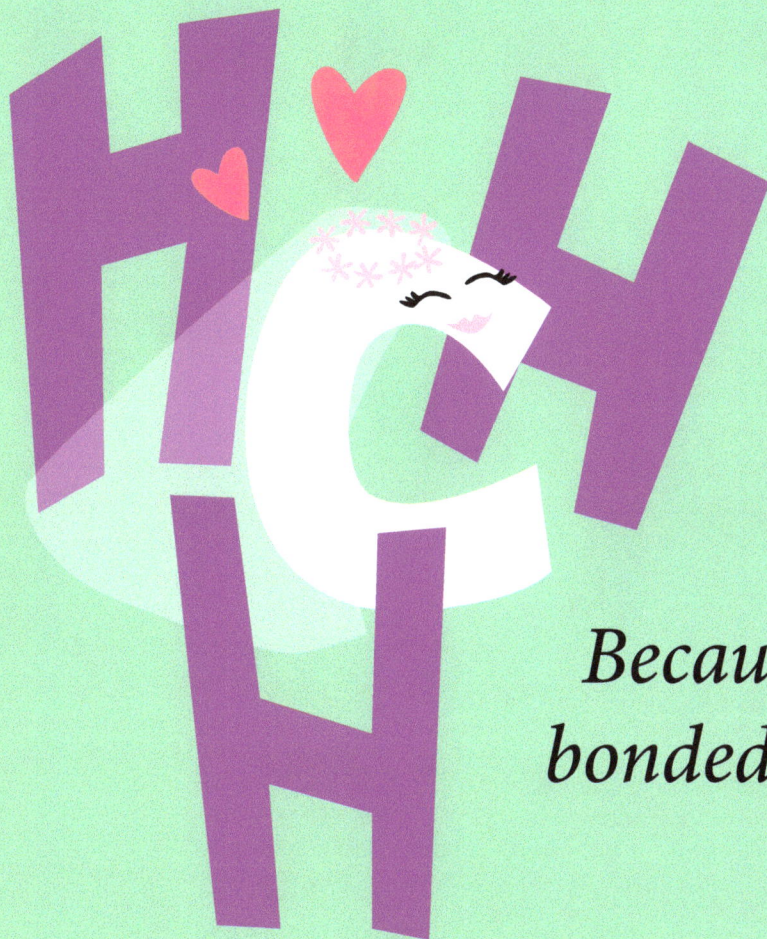

Because they bonded so well.

What's the first lesson you learn in chemistry?

Never lick the spoon.

What scientist does everyone listen to but never believe?

A meteorologist.

Knock, Knock!
Who's there?
Stopwatch!
Stopwatch who?

Stopwatch your doing
and pay attention to
the science teacher!

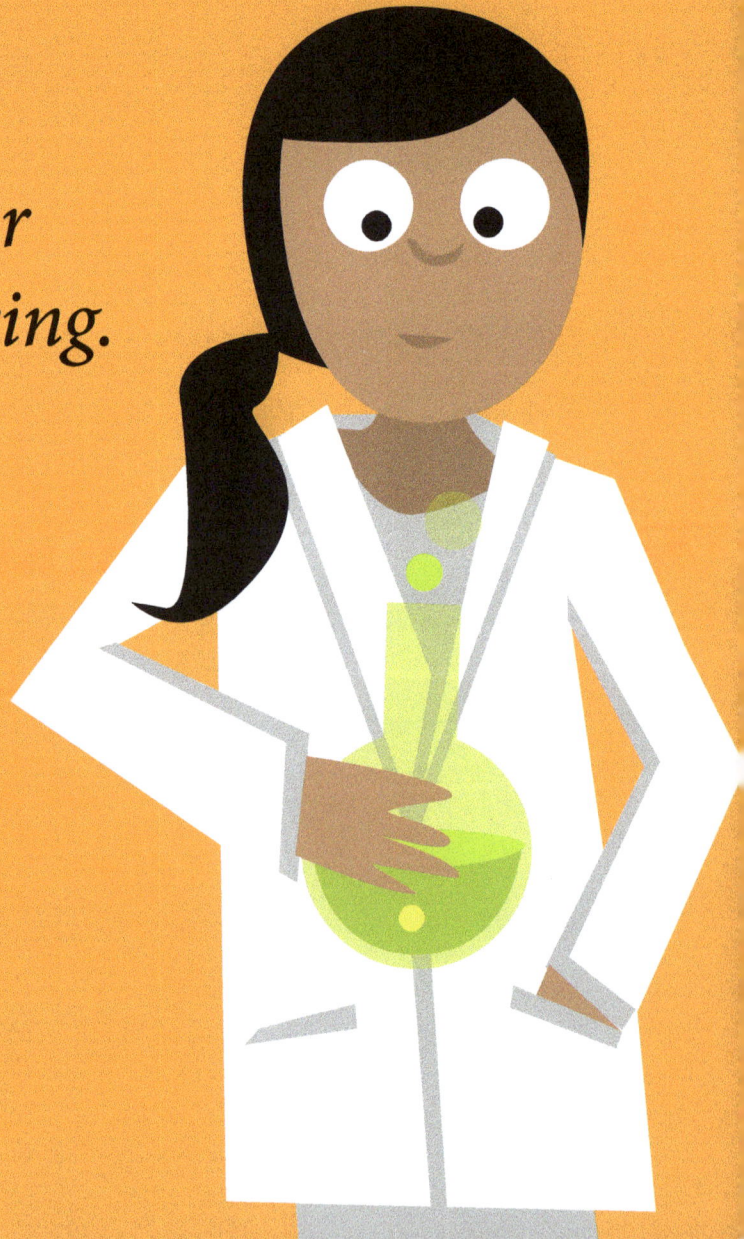

What happened to the chemistry joke?

There was no reaction.

www.ingramcontent.com/pod-product-compliance
Lightning Source LLC
LaVergne TN
LVHW070835080426

835508LV00031B/3477